DATE DUE

FOLLETT

World About Us

Deserts

By Harriet Brown

Stargazer Books

Designed and produced by
Aladdin Books Ltd

First published in the United States in 2007 by
Stargazer Books
c/o The Creative Company
123 South Broad Street
P.O. Box 227
Mankato, Minnesota 56002

Printed in the United States

Editor: Katie Harker

Design: Simon Morse
Flick, Book Design and Graphics

Picture researcher:
Alexa Brown

Illustrators:
James Field, Jonathan Latimer,
Rob Shone

Literacy consultant:
Jackie Holderness—former Senior Lecturer in Primary Education, Westminster Institute, Oxford Brookes University

Library of Congress Cataloging-in-Publication Data

Brown, Harriet.
Geography. Deserts /
by Harriet Brown.
p. cm. -- (World about us)
ISBN 978-1-59604-101-1
1. Deserts--Juvenile literature.
I. Title. II. World about us
(North Mankato, Minn.)

QH88.B74 2006
578.754--dc22

2005056717

CONTENTS

Notes to parents and teachers

This series has been developed for group use in the classroom, as well as for children reading alone. In particular, its text on two levels allows children of mixed abilities to enjoy reading about the same topic. The larger size text (A, below) offers apprentice readers a simplified text. This simplified text is used in the introduction to each chapter and in the picture captions. This font is part of the © Sassoon family of fonts whose maximum legibility is recommended for early readers. The smaller size text (B, below) offers a more challenging read for older or more able readers.

Deserts of the future

In the future, there could be more deserts than there are today. People are trying to stop the deserts from spreading.

A

◀ **Some countries are trying to stop the growth of deserts.**

Special farms have been set up in Israel to make the desert land more fertile. New plants have been added.

B

Questions, key words, and glossary

Each spread ends with a question that parents and teachers can use to discuss and develop further ideas and concepts. Further questions are provided in a quiz on page 30. A reduced version of pages 30 and 31 is shown below. The illustrated "Key words" section is provided as a revision tool, particularly for apprentice readers, in order to help with spelling, writing, and guided reading. The glossary is for more able or older readers.

In addition to the glossary's role as a reference aid, it is also designed to reinforce new vocabulary and provide a tool for further discussion and revision. When glossary terms first appear in the text, they are highlighted in bold.

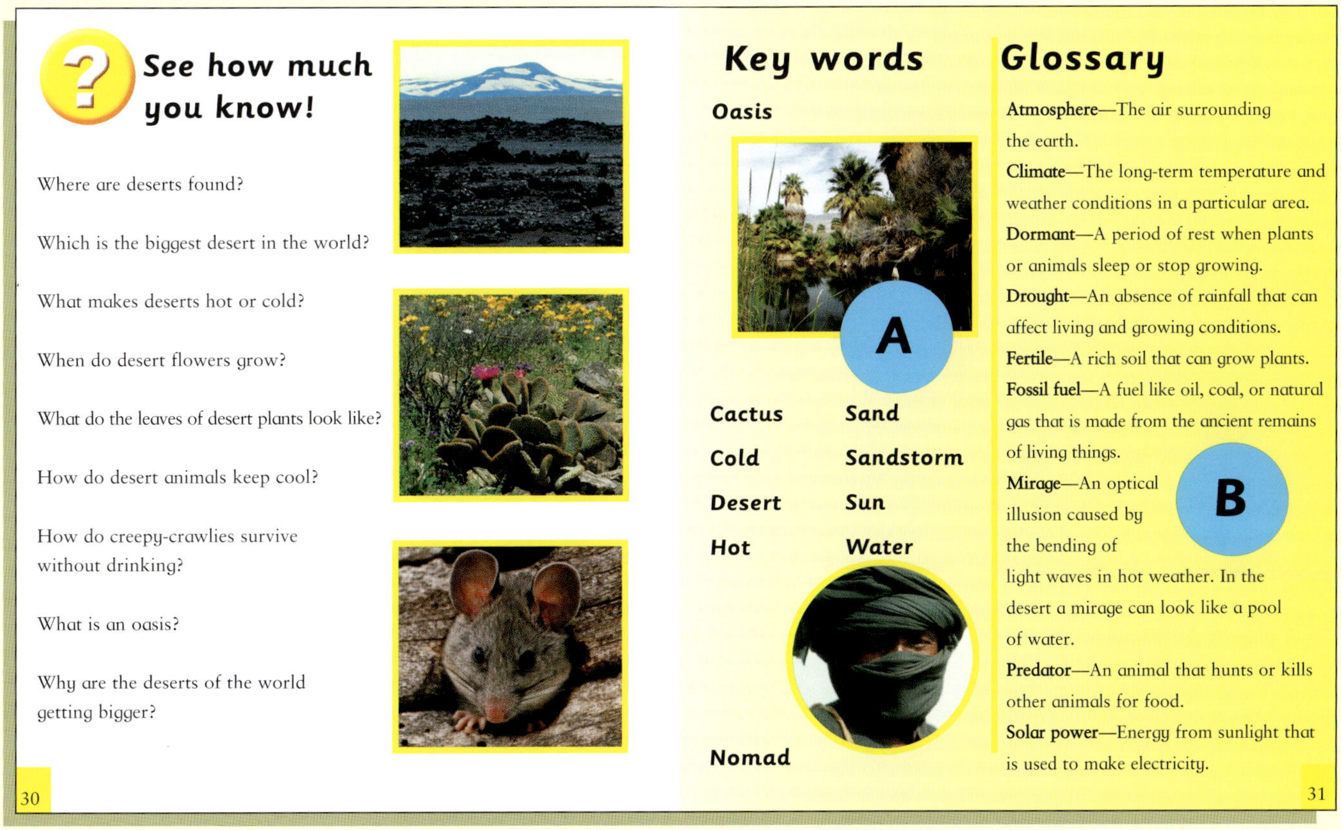

See how much you know!

Where are deserts found?

Which is the biggest desert in the world?

What makes deserts hot or cold?

When do desert flowers grow?

What do the leaves of desert plants look like?

How do desert animals keep cool?

How do creepy-crawlies survive without drinking?

What is an oasis?

Why are the deserts of the world getting bigger?

30

Key words

Oasis

A

Cactus
Cold
Desert
Hot
Sand
Sandstorm
Sun
Water
Nomad

Glossary

Atmosphere—The air surrounding the earth.
Climate—The long-term temperature and weather conditions in a particular area.
Dormant—A period of rest when plants or animals sleep or stop growing.
Drought—An absence of rainfall that can affect living and growing conditions.
Fertile—A rich soil that can grow plants.
Fossil fuel—A fuel like oil, coal, or natural gas that is made from the ancient remains of living things.
Mirage—An optical illusion caused by the bending of light waves in hot weather. In the desert a mirage can look like a pool of water.
Predator—An animal that hunts or kills other animals for food.
Solar power—Energy from sunlight that is used to make electricity.

B

31

What are deserts like?

Deserts are very dry places. They can be hot or cold. Deserts are found all across the world. Not all deserts are sandy. Some are covered with stones and rocks. Deserts don't have enough water for many plants to grow.

◀ A cold desert is a desert that has snow in the winter.

Cold deserts have snow in winter and a little rain in spring. They are always cold and even in spring and summer they do not get warm enough for most wildlife. Some grass and moss can grow, but most of the ground is covered with sand, rocks, and pebbles. Animals that live in cold deserts burrow into the ground to keep warm.

A hot desert can be cold at night.

Hot deserts absorb the heat of the sun during the day. At night, the heat escapes into the **atmosphere** because there are no clouds to prevent this. Temperatures can drop below freezing. Plants and animals have to cope with extreme temperatures every day.

Some of today's deserts used to be covered in grass.

African cave paintings in the Sahara Desert show animals walking in grass. Scientists think that a change of **climate** caused the plants to die. The soil became very dry and with no plants to hold it in place, the soil blew away.

? Why can't some plants grow in the desert?

Where are deserts?

Deserts cover around one-fifth of the earth and are found all over the planet. Hot deserts cover large parts of North and South America, Asia, Africa, and Australia. Cold deserts are mainly found at the poles, Greenland, parts of Asia, and North and South America.

◀ The Sahara Desert is in Africa.

The Sahara Desert is the largest desert in the world—almost as big as the whole of the U.S.! The central part is mountainous, but most of the Sahara is rocky and barren. Only about a third of it is sandy. Sand dunes in the Sahara can be up to 600 ft (180 m) tall—the same height as about 100 men!

This cold desert is in China.

The Taklamakan Desert is made of sand dunes and rocky soil. It is said that people who walk into this Chinese desert never return. There are freezing temperatures, many sandstorms, and poisonous creatures, like snakes.

This map shows the earth's deserts.

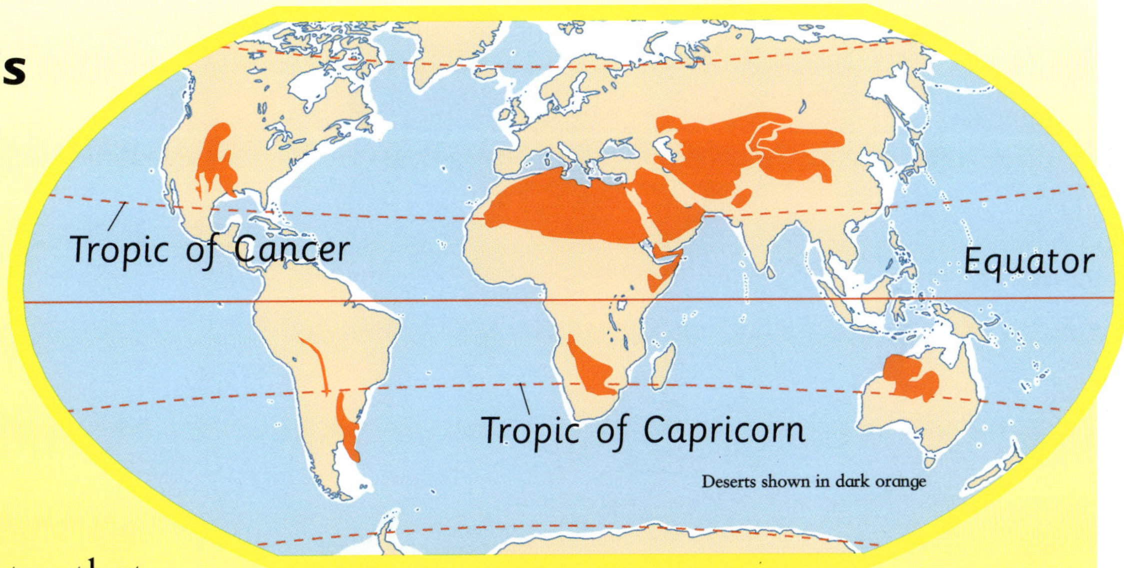

Around the middle of the earth is an imaginary line called the equator that separates the north from the south. The air at the equator contains lots of water so it rains a lot there. The Tropics of Capricorn and Cancer lie on each side of the equator where the air is very dry. This is where most hot deserts are found.

? How would you try to keep warm in a cold, icy desert?

Hot desert weather

Desert winds are strong and the air is dry. The heat in the desert is scorching during the day and freezing at night. Hot deserts have less than ten inches (25 cm) of rain each year, but sometimes this rain falls all at once.

◀ Thunderstorms can bring heavy rain.

Rain in the desert is torrential and can wash away soil and sand. If mountains are found near a desert, it may not rain for years. When air rises to pass over a mountain, the water vapor in the air cools and falls as rain. Once the air reaches the desert, there is no more rain to fall.

Desert rocks become very hot in the sun.

In a hot desert there are rarely clouds to block the heat of the sun. Air temperatures can reach 100°F (40°C) and the rocks and sand can be as hot as 160°F (70°C)—hot enough to fry an egg! Any moisture just evaporates.

Sandstorms blow sand around and hide the sun.

Strong winds whip up sand in the desert, and the air can become so thick with sand that it's difficult to breathe. The wind leaves ripples in the sand, like ripples on the surface of water. The sand is also carried for hundreds of miles by the wind.

? *Why does it sometimes not rain in the desert for years?*

Spikes and leaves

Not many plants and trees grow in the desert. Those that can survive there have spikes instead of leaves. Spikes lose less water than flat leaves. They also stop desert animals from eating the leaves. Some desert trees have very long roots to collect as much water as possible.

◀ Trees and shrubs grow in stony deserts.

Acacia trees are widespread in parts of the Sahara and Australian deserts. To survive the extreme summer heat, desert trees lose their leaves and even their branches to stop growing and become **dormant**. They dry out completely and although they look dead they still produce flowers and leaves when the rains come.

Desert flowers grow when it rains.

Flowers can suddenly grow in the desert when it rains. The plants grow quickly to produce seeds ready for when it rains again. Shallow ground roots help desert plants to access rainwater quickly.

Cacti are full of juice.

The cactus is the most famous desert plant. Cacti survive in hot deserts by storing water in their thick stems. The saguaro cactus, found in Arizona's Sonoran Desert, has roots that spread in a circle around the cactus. They wrap around rocks to hold the cactus upright in strong winds.

How do cacti protect themselves from thirsty desert animals?

How animals keep cool

Many animals, such as rats, foxes, and camels, live in the desert. Desert animals try to keep cool. Some live underground to stay out of the heat, or only come out at night. Desert animals have also adapted to live in the heat.

◀ **Most desert rats wake up to hunt at night.**

One of the best ways that desert animals avoid the heat of the sun is to be **nocturnal**. They sleep during the day and become active at night. Most desert rats are nocturnal. They live in cool underground burrows.

Pale fur keeps these desert fox cubs cool.

Many desert animals are pale to reflect the sun's rays. Others lose heat through the large surface area of their ears. The fennec fox is well adapted to desert life with pale skin and large ears. Other creatures, like kangaroos, lick themselves to keep cool.

Camels can wait nearly a week for a drink of water.

A camel can live for days without drinking because its blood is designed to hold extra water. Camels have another clever way of keeping cool. Their body temperature is colder than the desert air so they huddle together to keep cool.

Why are small feet useful when walking on hot sand?

Water creatures

Deserts are very dry places. In some deserts there is water only after heavy rainfall. In other deserts there is some water all year round, in rivers, pools, or oases. The animals that live in the water have special ways of coping with desert life.

▼ Desert dragonflies hatch near a water source.

Dragonflies are found near desert ponds. Adult dragonflies scatter their eggs over the water or on plants near to an oasis (see page 25). Their eggs hatch into larvae. After a few months the larvae crawl out of the water where they slowly emerge from their shell. Most adult dragonflie live for only a few months.

Desert pupfish live in mud pools.

Pupfish live in the Mojave Desert, which covers southeast California and portions of Nevada, Arizona, and Utah. In winter they hibernate at the bottom of desert pools, but in the spring they mate and lay eggs. Pupfish can withstand the desert heat, but most die when their pools dry up in summer.

Some desert frogs store water under their skin.

To stay moist, the Australian water-storing frog burrows into the ground and wraps a cocoon of dead skin around itself to store pockets of water. The frog can stay like that until the next wet period, which may not be for years!

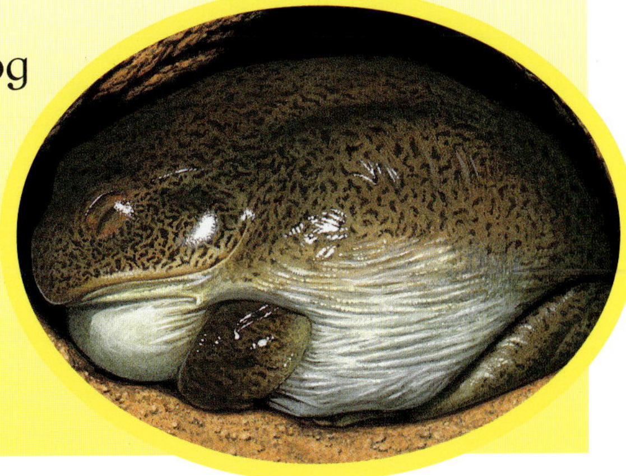

How do frogs usually stay moist?

Desert birds

Birds find it easier to survive in the desert than other animals. This is because they can fly away to look for food or water. Desert birds that can't fly very well often have nests on the ground and are good at running.

◀ **These owls live in underground burrows.**

Burrowing owls are found throughout the deserts of the U.S. They generally live in cool underground burrows that have been dug by other animals, such as prairie dogs or rodents. Occasionally, they dig their own burrow. The burrowing owl does not need a thick layer of feathers.

Roadrunners store energy when they sleep.

On cold nights, roadrunners save energy by going into a kind of hibernation, where they can't move or feel anything. Instead of using up energy trying to stay warm, they bask in the sun in the morning to warm up.

The world's biggest bird, the ostrich, lives in Africa.

Ostriches live in the African deserts. They can grow as tall as a man and their eyeballs can be two inches (5 cm) across. Ostriches can't fly, but they can run very fast.

? Which other animals do you know that live in a burrow?

Creepy-crawlies

Creepy-crawlies, such as insects and spiders, are well suited to life in the desert. They have a hard skeleton on the outside of their bodies that traps moisture inside the body. Most creepy-crawlies don't need to drink at all. They get enough water from their food.

◀ Scarab beetles hide their eggs in dung.

Female scarab beetles hide their eggs in balls of dung to protect them from **predators**. The eggs remain in the dung, which the female pushes around, until they hatch. The Ancient Egyptians thought that scarab beetles were sacred because they "came to life."

Desert spiders are big.

Desert spiders tend to be large so that they can keep more water in their bodies. Instead of using webs, desert spiders tend to hunt their prey on the ground. They keep out of the heat by hiding under rocks or by burrowing.

Scorpions cope with desert life better than any other creepy-crawly.

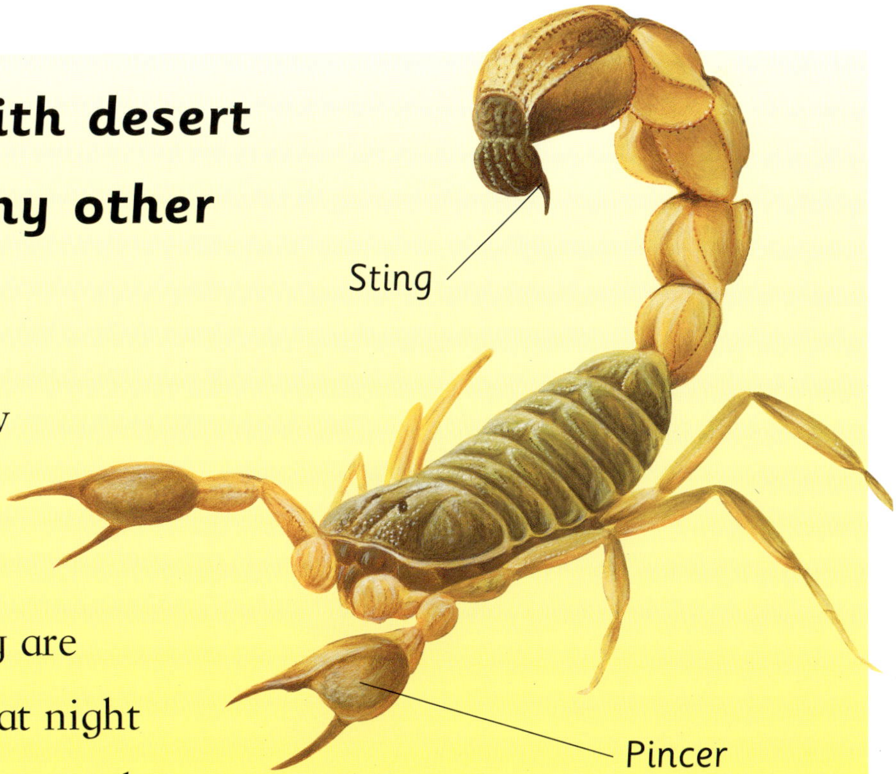

Scorpions have a very low rate of water loss and spend most of the day asleep underground. They are carnivores and come out at night to hunt prey, such as insects and spiders. They grab their victim in their pincers and paralyze it with their poisonous sting.

? Why don't spiders build webs in the desert?

Snakes and lizards

Snakes and lizards are coldblooded reptiles. They cannot make their own heat (like mammals can) but are the same temperature as their surroundings. During the day, coldblooded animals are warmed up by the heat of the sun.

◀ **Rattlesnakes shake their tails to warn other animals to stay away.**

Rattlesnakes hunt animals that they can swallow whole, such as small rodents and rabbits. Some rattlesnakes hunt at night, but others are happy to hunt during the heat of the day. Rattlesnakes try to avoid predators like roadrunner birds who eat them.

Some lizards stand on two legs to keep their feet cool.

Desert lizards often have long legs to keep their body far away from the hot rocks or sand. Some species rest most of their body weight on their heels so that only a small area of their feet is on the ground.

Horned lizards blow themselves up with air to scare their enemies.

Horned lizards are dragon-like creatures that live in the deserts of North America. If they are caught they blow themselves up with air, to look big and dangerous. They have also been known to squirt blood from the corners of their eyes!

? Why can't a snake stay in the sun for a long time?

People of the desert

Desert people try to live near a water source. Sometimes they catch the water from fog or morning dew using special sheets. Some desert people are called "nomads" because they move from place to place. They carry or find all the supplies they need to build shelters.

◀ **Desert people wear special clothes.**

To avoid the heat, desert people wear clothing that covers them from head to toe. Long-flowing robes prevent skin from burning and allow the air to circulate to keep their skin cool. Clothes are also used to keep sand from blowing into the eyes and mouth.

◀ An oasis is a fertile area with a water source.

Desert people often stop at **fertile** oases to find water for their animals to drink. People also set up homes in oases. Las Vegas is built on an oasis in the Great Basin Desert.

The desert can play tricks with your eyes.

Traveling through the desert can be dangerous. You may become lost if a sandstorm changes the landscape. You may also see a pool of water that isn't there. When the sun heats the desert floor, the air above warms up and causes the light to bend. You see a reflection of the sky on this hot layer of air, that looks like water. This is called a "**mirage**."

? What would happen if you tried to reach a mirage?

Changing deserts

Many desert lands are rich in oil. Oil is formed from the remains of plants and animals that lived millions of years ago. Deserts also contain minerals and fossils. Deserts change naturally over time, but humans affect deserts too.

◀ **Global warming is causing deserts to form.**

When **fossil fuels** are burned to make electricity, they release a gas called carbon dioxide into the atmosphere. This prevents heat from escaping the earth and causes our climate to warm up. In some parts of the world, global warming is causing a **drought** and more land is turning into dry deserts. This is called "desertification."

People dig for diamonds in the desert.

Many deserts are important sources of precious rocks and minerals. Diamonds form over millions of years, deep beneath the earth's surface where there is crushing pressure and blistering heat.

Dinosaur fossils are found in the desert.

Fossils are the remains of plants and animals that have been preserved in stone. The Patagonia Desert in Argentina has remains of Tyrannosaurus rex, one of the largest meat-eaters ever discovered. Tyrannosaurus rex roamed the deserts over 150 million years ago.

? What will the deserts look like in a thousand years?

Deserts of the future

In the future, there could be more deserts than there are today. People are trying to stop the deserts from spreading. Some people are planting special trees and plants to try to turn the deserts back into fertile land. Others think we can use the deserts more effectively.

◀ **Some countries are trying to stop the growth of deserts.**

Special farms have been set up in Israel to make the desert land more fertile. New plants have been added to encourage plant growth. These plants come from other deserts where they grow well in the dry soil. Watering also helps to grow crops in these dry areas.

◀ Deserts are good places to catch energy from the sun.

Solar power changes the sun's energy into electricity. Deserts are ideal places to build solar farms because there are few clouds and lots of sunlight. A remote area in the Qizilqum Desert in Uzbekistan in Asia now has electricity for the first time, thanks to solar power.

This waste may cause harm to desert animals.

Some people think that deserts are ideal places to store waste from cities and factories because very few people live there. Waste can be stored beneath the desert floor but if it is not properly managed it can pollute the land and water, endangering wildlife.

How could we make the deserts more fertile?

See how much you know!

Where are deserts found?

Which is the biggest desert in the world?

What makes deserts hot or cold?

When do desert flowers grow?

What do the leaves of desert plants look like?

How do desert animals keep cool?

How do creepy-crawlies survive without drinking?

What is an oasis?

Why are the deserts of the world getting bigger?

Key words

Oasis

Cactus

Cold

Desert

Hot

Sand

Sandstorm

Sun

Water

Nomad

Glossary

Atmosphere—The air surrounding the earth.

Climate—The long-term temperature and weather conditions in a particular area.

Dormant—A period of rest when plants or animals sleep or stop growing.

Drought—An absence of rainfall that can affect living and growing conditions.

Fertile—A rich soil that can grow plants.

Fossil fuel—A fuel like oil, coal, or natural gas that is made from the ancient remains of living things.

Mirage—An optical illusion caused by the bending of light waves in hot weather. In the desert, a mirage can look like a pool of water.

Nocturnal—Being active at night.

Predator—An animal that hunts or kills other animals for food.

Solar power—Energy from sunlight that can be used to make electricity.

Index

Photocredits:

Abbreviations: l-left, r-right, b-bottom, t-top, c-center, m-middle

Front cover, 5lt, 6bl, 26bl, 29br, 30t — Photo Disc Images. Back cover, 5rt, 25tl, 31t — www.istockphoto.com / Rich Tull. 1, 3mt, 8tl, 10tr, 10bl, 12bl, 14tr — Corbis. 2-3, 3t, 3mb, 5l 5lb, 5rb, 6tr, 8bl, 9t, 11bl, 12tl, 13tl, 13br, 14bl, 15tr, 15bl, 16tl, 19tr, 19bl, 22tr, 22bl, 24tl, 24bl, 27tr, 30m, 30b, 32b — Corel. 3b — www.istockphoto.com / Juliana Halvorson. 4t – www.istockphoto.com / Perttu Sironen. 4b, 28bl — thanks to Sergy Kravchenko. 7tr — www.istockphoto.com / Tomasz Resiak. 7bl — www.istockphoto.com / William McKelvie. 11tr www.istockphoto.com / Sean McBride.16bl, 26tr, 29tl — Digital Vision Photos. 17t — Garold W Sneegas.18tr — John Foxx Photos. 18bl — Copyright 2004 Steve Berliner. 20tl — Ot Rogge Photography. 20bl — Jaci's Safari Lodge www.madikwe.com. 21tl — www.istockphoto.com / Juliana Halvorson. 23tr — www.istockphoto.com / Ceuleers Johan. 23bl — www.istockphoto.com / Kevin Tate. 25br — Copyright © 2003 by Ctein. 28tl — www.istockphoto.com / Perttu Sironen.